KU-545-846

GERI

First published in Great Britain in 1997 by Reed Children's Books
a division of Reed International Books Ltd.
Michelin House, 81 Fulham Road, London SW3 6RB, Auckland and Melbourne
Devised by Beth Wyllyams, Mandy Norman and Linda Males
Text and design copyright © Reed International Books Ltd.
Dedicated to Alice Hardie-Grant
Printed in Great Britain
ISBN 0 7497 3309 8

1 3 5 7 9 10 8 6 4 2

Geri (short for Geraldine) Estelle Halliwell, known to the world as Ginger Spice, was born on 6th August 1972 in Watford.

WHO IS GERI?

She is 5ft 1in tall with blue eyes and her trademark red hair.

What she lacks in height, she more than makes up for in personality: along with Mel B, Geri is the loudest Spice Girl!

Geri's distinguishing marks include a pierced bellybutton, tattoos of a Jaguar and a sundial on her back and very big shoes!

3

EARLY MEMORIES

Geri is the youngest of five children. Her mum, Andrea, is Spanish and Geri is also one quarter Swedish.

Geri's mum is very proud of Geri and the Spice Girls' huge success!

Geri went to an all-girls school. She hated the uniform and all the rules.

After she left school, she had an amazing number of different jobs.

She has been a hairdresser, an aerobics teacher, a sales assistant, a club dancer in Majorca and even a game show hostess on Turkish TV!

GERI'S ROLE IN THE BAND

Unlike the other Spices, Geri is not a trained singer or dancer.

But she was determined to be a part of the **Spice Girls**. She knew that she could use her strong personality to bring some extra spirit to the group, and kept on phoning the management team.

Pretty soon Geri persuaded them that she was exactly what they were looking for.

The other Spices tease Geri about being **bossy**, but she says that really it's just because she's the organised one!

She has led a **wild and varied life**, so she's never short of new ideas for the Spices' songs.

Geri came up with the name for the band!

PERSONALITY PROFILE

Geri describes herself as a 'rebel with a cause'. Her cause is **Girl Power**.

She hates narrow-mindedness and loves to shock.

Geri is very talkative with a **big** personality, but she has a thoughtful, serious side too.

Always outspoken, she believes that it is important to stand up for what you think is right.

Geri says that she has always been independent, living on her wits and talking people into letting her do the things she wants to do.

When people tell her she can't do something, it just makes her even more determined to succeed.

She is full of energy and needs lots of new challenges to stop her from getting bored, **including scary things like cross-country skiing and ballooning!**

Geri's heroes are people with principles.

GERI'S ROLE MODELS

She caused quite a stir when she claimed that **Margaret Thatcher**, the first woman British prime minister, is a role model for the Spice Girls. ★

"Thatcher was the first Spice Girl, the pioneer of our ideology," she told highbrow magazine <u>The Spectator</u>.

Although Geri doesn't agree with all her views, she respects her for standing up and saying what she believes in.

AMBITIONS

Geri has always been determined to be famous, and when she sets her heart on something, she never gives up.

She will settle for nothing less than world domination for the Spices — and her dream seems to be coming true!

Geri wants everyone to get the Girl Power message.

Geri's other wish is to drive a really posh car.

When the Spices hit the big time, she bought an **MGB 1967 Roadster convertible** with silver spokes, like the car which appears in the classic James Bond movies.

"The engine sounds like my voice when I've been out all night," says Geri.

STYLE

Geri's style is glamorous, with a funky seventies twist.

She occasionally buys clothes from high-street shops, but her sister makes a lot of clothes for her.

She also likes to buy from markets and second hand shops.

Geri says that she dresses to suit how she's feeling each day.

Her clothes reflect her **mood**!

But above all, for Geri, dressing up should be fun!

All the Spices say that when they first met Geri, they thought she was a complete "**nutter**"!

Emma **particularly remembers her big shoes and** Victoria **says that she'd never met anyone who dresses quite like Geri!**

THE SPICES ON GERI!

Geri is so lively, she needs lots of attention from her friends.

Emma says Geri gives good advice and is great for partying with!

Mel B says that Geri is very good to talk to, although she's very full of her own opinions!

SPICE QUIZ!

So now you've read all about **Geri** but how much can you remember? Check your Spice knowledge with these questions. ••••••

(Answers at the bottom of the page.)

1 What nationality is Geri's mum?

2 What quality did Geri believe she could bring to the Spice Girls?

3 What job did Geri have on Turkish TV?

4 According to Geri, who was the first Spice Girl?

5 What did Geri buy after the Spice Girls became famous?

Answers: 1 Spanish, 2 Spirit, 3 A gameshow hostess, 4 Margaret Thatcher, 5 A really posh car